The Woman You

Think I Am

poems by

Karen Nelson

[handwritten inscription: "much love to a delightful young woman & friend ... 12/05 to Chris — I love my "Rocking Southwestern Sensuality" enjoy with joy Karen"]

Acknowledgements

The following poems first appeared in the publications cited:

Branches	*I Don't Understand*
Buffalo Bones	*No More Mine*
Earth's Daughters	*Michael's Letter*
The Larcom Review	*The World Over*
Poetry Motel	*I Shout*
Poet's Touchstone	*Dutiful Husband*
	He Married Her
	for the Second Time

Cover art painting: Kate Nelson
Cover: John Magnifico
Karen's photograph: Bob Nelson

Northwoods Press
The Poets' Press
Thomaston, Maine 04861

Contents

Dedication

I dedicate this book to two poets of the next generation who, at ages 8 and 7, wrote the following:

Plums
by Kate Nelson — 2000

Picking plums is fun
gold and silver plums
the song of the plums
the tale of the happiness
the plums glide so sweetly
on the trees of the branch
the branches are lightly
and sweet color of the song

Love
by Carl-Robert Nelson — 2004

Love is a drifting,
going across the trees of spring.
Love is why you are here.
It's like a heart that doesn't stop beating,
or a flower that doesn't stop growing.
If nobody loved each other,
love would just be history.

One

Marriage

Your words sting like radishes
on my tongue.
I slice them for supper,
count others in the bunch.
Roots trail from the end of each.
Red fades to pink and white.
I am so close to leaving you
I can see the distance between
my two fingers, the width
of one small radish,
easy to lift from the earth.

Chafe / Chaff

to irritate or wear away remains, hulls, rubbish

How we used to chafe against
the things not like us,
wanting to erase any reminder

of your callousness
and my greed.
Rubbing away by irritating,

fretting to get rid of
what annoyed us 惘
We couldn't stand another day

vexing and abrading
the things we didn't find
in ourselves.

Chafing against each other
to find the grain,
a kernel of something

growing in an open field,
seared, hardened, made hardhearted
by the sun.

Didn't we know that this
annoying gnawing at
our stronger points

left only
glumes and husks
of a prior we?

What we considered of no value
because it didn't gleam
kernel-like in us

we've worn away now,
one body against the other,
leaving limbs loosely

hanging, dried husks flapping
like so many scarecrows
after the corn has been picked.

We Stop Our Bitter Fights

One morning after your bath
you lie back on the covers,
pull me down beside you,

let your fingers slide gently
as you point out tiny canary-like birds
in the silk-oak trees outside our window,

their shrill music
a back beat to our hum and purr.
I watch your damp body beside me,

admire the way buttocks curve into thighs,
the rounding where the hollow of my hand
fits your flesh.

We settle into mounds of cotton,
wrinkled curves and crevices,
another sleepy afternoon.

Hear the house settle down to itself.
The hall door creaks on a hinge that never works,
our cocker's toenails click on tile.

Our limbs contract, relax in time.
I continue my lifelong intrigue
with your body's smell:

zucchini picked fresh from our garden,
mixture of soap--musk and orange blossom--
this aroma of places where we used to make love

near animal tracks,
by orange groves along the road,
a place to retreat.

I Shout

A coyote yells at the moon,
knows what her shouts mean—
her promises
fill every mouthful.

I shout my wild orgasmic shouts
to the coyotes who have just finished chomping
a rib bone tossed to them by me, the woman
who shouts.

All women must scream the noises
rising in their throats
from places that roar,
where dark voices hide.

Howls that lie at the well's bottom
are not something sweet or good
for a man to stumble onto on his way down
or in.

A wild coyote cries on a mountain top;
a three-quarters moon shapes her belly.

Nordic

"The men from Northern Europe
can't talk about their feelings"
you always tell me.
My Armenian side wants to wake you
from your slumber,
wants to dance naked
in the streets of Leucadia,
lean out windows
high up in New York skyscrapers,
breasts resting on old brick ledges
to welcome the first snow.
Your Nordic habit,
cold, self-contained--
a resting cat who ignores
the frisky cocker who circles more than once.

When we married I thought I could
break your Nordic spell.
I danced around you at Western cabarets,
bluegrass festivals,
flaunting my cape,
flinging it out in all directions.

Going to bed with you is another story.
There, you let me strip away that slumber
like clothing from your body.
At the sight of you
my breath catches in my throat,
lets itself out with a whistle.
I dance a Balkan circle
and wake you with my Armenian tongue.

Early Morning

You nuzzle me, rooting around
in the bedclothes,
searching for your truffle.

We both know
what you are looking for.
I tease you by evasion,
then produce what you most covet,

guiding your mouth to my nipple.
Afterwards, we lie with our bodies' lengths
curved into each other's hollows,
cuddling before the new day.

You say my skin's softness
arouses a memory
about rabbits
nestled in hollows,
safe from the red-tailed hawk.

Summer Morning

You've gone inside to fix an omelet
with avocados, fresh tomatoes,
slivers of parmesan to please the Italian in me.
One hummingbird zings near the pewter-colored wind chimes.

My friend said here you can lie outside
naked, and no one will see you.
Off with my white eyelet dress!
Lovers in Sicily don't cover up —
the hummer swoops in over my head for nectar.

Sun over desert hills
warms the back of my knees
with a light touch in their hollow place.
Willow lounge chair imprints my back.
No eyes but red-shouldered hawks' for miles.
Boulder outcrops glazed blank in the sun's heat.

Plate in hand, you walk gingerly
across uneven flagstone
talking about our gourmet cooking—
\sautéed onions, sweet tomatoes.
You stop — take a step back,
gaze longingly.
A thirty year flashback to our wedding night.
Then, I wouldn't undress in the light.

Moosehead Lake

Thirty years ago, we docked
at the edge of Lake Maligne,
climbed up the slight incline,
lay down in grass.
Two moose ambled over.
You whispered
while my back crunched leaves.
Wild things, all four of us.
They wild for what they fed on.
We wild for what we knew.
Your musky aroma
called me to you,
crunch of leaves underneath.
Moose sauntered away through tunneled forest.

Today,
two young moose
partially hidden by orange-gold trees
frosted with yesterday's snow,
ambling and placid,
grins on their faces,
spied in the light
of an early Maine sunrise.

They nuzzle,
rub shoulder to shoulder,
sniff winter coming:
smell apple rinds, cranberries, wet, moist;
sugar maples, leaves dropping, becoming
compost, yellow on top, deep brown
almost black underneath.

Your Averted Gaze

As I talk to your often admired profile,
I stop in mid-sentence.
                    My hand reaches for your cheek,
turns your face toward mine,
holds your gaze
with my quiet, level stare.
When your eyes veer away
mine track you.
You shift, avoid my gaze.
I want the mating dance of the eyes,
to lock gaze with you.
Instead, as male elk do
we lock horns.

Flesh Never Gives Up

It longs for,
desires often,
outright shouts.
Some days
all its owner can do
is listen.

And it has its expectations.
It must be fed, washed,
waved at and read to.
It craves back rubs,
aromatherapy,
orgasmic relief.
Sluggish and damp
it clings
to yours.

Falling to sleep,
you always
want to drape
your thigh
over mine.
I can't stand
the weight
and how
it sticks to me.

Yacqui Well

Bumble bees' furry bodies
circle, crisscross
around cattails and reeds,
weave black and gold,
cattail brown.
Frantic desire for water
propels two wings,
one head, six legs
toward the stagnant mud
of an old Indian well.
We propel our bodies
toward each other.

Wheat Germ, Oat Bran, Brewers Yeast
Raisins, Apricots, Dates, Some Applesauce,
Milk And The Bee Pollen

If you decide
to climb inside
this hive of goodness
and munch
whole wheat kernels
the words
you have to wade through
eat, forget, me,
hollow

glistening ochre
on your spoon
the layers of another poem
 macabre,
sensuous, gliding
aphrodisiac, swan

Mesopotamia's
gardens
where bee pollen
grows and glows
vibrate, munch,
crunch

Holding On

to the escalator
of sleep
going down, down
while he pinches
my bun between thumb
and forefinger,
massaging gently,
not letting go.
I let go easily,
hoping to glide gently
into petals on a pond
of remembrance.

A Love Story

"They join each other in a ceremony, and this union of two slices is called marriage. Even together the two do not make up one person!" Robert Bly

Once there was
a young woman with mourning eyes,
and a sorrow-faced man
who came to the altar.

Heavy potato sacks
on their backs
weighed them down.

"I do." "I will." After their vows,
they hitchhiked from the church
to San Francisco
where they became lost

trying to find a hotel for the night.
They thought a malicious giant
had removed all the street signs
except for the ones that said

NO LEFT TURN.
He brought his family's lie
to the room with him.
At twelve his grandma said

"The woman who comes
on Sundays
is your mother,
not your sister."

She brought her family's secret
in a flowerpot. When her father
died, her mother hid
every picture of him

and swept her playroom

with quick, decisive turns
of the broom.
She thought he might be

her "dream daddy," and she
would put his picture
above her bed.
He was thinking she

could be his lost mother
if he held her close enough,
squeezed her rib bones hard
into the concave below his chest.

They lived in many houses
but made love in only one,
in the living room,
on Christmas Eve

after he gave her the brass pendant
with tiny Mexican soap opals.
He breathed kisses up her body,
only penetrated her

when she began her soft,
low moans, the doves' litany
at sundown
in the San Joaquin

near the green pastures where he was born.
Years later she left on a journey
to retrieve all the sunlight
he had sucked from her.

She returned home one Sunday
to lay down with him.
Did she thank a slice of herself for guessing
when to leave and when to return?

Two

Michael's Letter

From San Quentin State Prison
Death Row

"A child said what is the grass?" Walt Whitman

Today in his letter
he told us
about a trip he made one evening
to the law library.

A guard took him
after dark,
the night of the full moon,
light he could see

streaming down
onto concrete walkways
between buildings,
onto grass.

It lit a small patch
between brick prison walls.
"Can I stand on the grass?"
he asked the guard

He went on to tell us
how he took off his shoes,
stepped gingerly onto something
green and soft

he hadn't touched
for almost ten years.
He felt like crying, he said,
wanted to bend down

and smell the sweet stuff,
but he shifted from one foot
to the next, he wrote,
feeling the moist blades
between his toes.

He watched moonlight fall
from above,
fall on his face,
fall on his handcuffs,
leg irons,
fall on the green
where he stood.

A Don Lino Afternoon

Sunday afternoon, my husband smokes a Don Lino
on the front porch of his mom's mobile home.
Wind chimes bloom, red camellias zing.
My legs propped
on his Levi-covered thighs,
I hear the sound of metal on glass next door,
guessing eggs or milk beaten for custard.

I've just finished a piece of coconut cream pie.
Mid-afternoon sun rays
across the nearest mobile home
at a right angle to carpeted moss-green stairs,
bends down to intersect wrought iron.

Don Lino smoke blends
spice with almond orchards
on Sunday afternoon.
White ash builds a blossom pyramid.

Amy Asked Her Father His Favorite Places

as in locations, for making love.
There was Toroweap, Grand Canyon National Monument.
Two bodies stretched flat on a mesa bared
to the August moon. One sleeping bag warmed cold granite.

"You didn't," she giggled. "Yes," he said.

Then Lake Maligne, British Columbia, Canada.
The boat ride to the other side of the lake,
a brief hike through underbrush to a clearing.
Two moose who sauntered over to watch.

"No, I can't believe it," she gasped. "Yes," he said.

Camp Pendleton, a spread of dry, summer-golden grass
hot to the touch--we pulled off the road,
nestled in the weeds' warmth, wondered if recruits
might march by.

"Not Camp Pendleton! I know someone stationed there!"
"Yes," he said.

"Then Anza Borrego. Your favorite
place, Amy, 110 degrees in July." "Yeah, right, Dad."
It was your Mother's birthday. We walked among desert lilies
near an underground spring.

"That's some of them," he said.

The Snake House

Sun plays through the jacaranda
against my slank body,
shadows the fern-like branches across an arm.
They flatten against the wind.
Close voices rustle
like dry pods.
A buzz saw
splinters the afternoon.
My husband and son are building
a snake-house.
Father leans over
to show his boy
where to pound the nails.
As they draw near,
I shed my fragile skin.

Driving 405 South

On my car radio a woman speaks--
"My Mother couldn't help what she did; she
didn't want to hurt us." And the doctor
tells her: "Your Mother made choices--
don't let her off the hook."

The day of Daddy's funeral
I was ten years old.
I watched from the four-poster bed
where they slept before my daddy died.
Zoe, her best friend, hugged her.
They didn't see me. Mother, with her page boy haircut,
leaned into Zoe's silky blouse
the way I wanted to press against Mother.

"Your mother made choices."

She hid the pictures of my father
while I stuffed grief like cotton balls
inside my mouth.

After that, she spent most days
in the burgundy wing chair,
staring at Oregon street.
Didn't rouse herself enough to flick a leaf.

Her litany: "Get my sweater,
make some coffee; talk to your
brother, he won't talk to me.
Where shall we move to--?"

She drank the bitterness
of daddy's leukemia, held the cup
to her lips the way she held it to mine
when I was small.

"Don't let her off the hook"
Looking for men she went dancing.

I woke to voices outside my bedroom.
She fed them sandwiches and coffee.

One was twenty years younger. Two she married after
knowing them six weeks, one she divorced. The other she stayed
with, denied. He told her when she was old her "karma" would
haunt her. The other came to my bedroom and stroked me,
left when satisfied.

"Your Mother could help it."

The sun glazes my arm resting on the edge
of the car door.
A glimpse of light out of the corner of my eye,
an arm lit with a few sparse hairs--
what the truth looks like.

"You can live with the truth."

Chapultapec Castle

A tall, lean Aztec leaves the mural,
and takes her arm.

    She allows him.
    He knows she will come.

They sit facing each other in a brown leather booth.
    She orders café con leche
    in a pitcher.
Aztec pulls her foot towards him.
His hand cradles her instep, her arch,
her foot's link with earth, leaves.
He massages each toe, tastes them.
Putting one inside his mouth,
he arouses a memory of her stepfather's touch.
He was there stroking her thighs, satisfying himself.
She pictures blood on the castle's ceiling.

Her mother brought men home, fed them
in the breakfast nook outside her bedroom door.
Waking to various voices rising on Friday
and Saturday nights.

In an old dream she hears her mother speak:

    "I'm not complete.
    I'm half a woman without a man."

Too late she pulls away.

The Wing Chair

She would sit for hours in a wine-colored wing chair,
staring outside. Years later she said she missed me
growing up with friends on Oregon street.

When I came back for something I'd forgotten,
she couldn't see me. The upholstery
encompassed her body. I thought those wings

belonged to angels who protected her,
enclosing Mother in red feathers
where she sang inside with them.

What I didn't know was that she entertained
the devil, played with her thoughts like dominoes,
white spots her only point of hope,

an escape route
for a mind that always played to the dark.
Each thought she placed on her tongue,

where it left just enough bitterness toward God
to savor the next morning. On Saturdays, my brother Ray and I
would play monopoly. We didn't see her

until she popped out of her bedroom at noon,
drugged with sleep, wondering what we were up to.
We had already bought dozens of properties,

mortgaged ourselves to the hilt,
before she climbed out from under the covers.
I waited from sixth grade through high school

for her to notice that I hadn't died with Daddy.
Running in breathless from flying on my flexie,
gliding down Berkeley's hills, going

to Manuel's for candy, Neccoes and red vines.
I slipped from room to room calling her name,
forgetting about the angel chair and its wing

which hid her from me.
Once I fell against it, bumped the wing.
Her gaze still fixed on the road, eyes glazed,

while I bounced a ball beside her.
Inside my head I heard her say,
I'm so glad you came to talk with me.

Before I could answer, she ended our interview.
While I ran outdoors into the sun,
she settled back into the dark,

rested one cheek against a wing,
a gesture that ferried her to Daddy's grave
where she'd lean in all afternoon.

I'm Not The Woman You Think I Am

efficient, mean and glazed--
ornery trickster with a tricks bag,
someone for you to laugh
at, but

never emulate.
I'm not
smooth enough to swallow like
homemade kahluas, or the hugger and pleaser

you've come to know and expect.
I won't be there with ready answers,
a constant smile.
I want something you're not prepared to give.

I'm the woman who snores, sucks ice cream, pulls
socks and shoes off at a moment's notice, laughs
with a snort like her mother, speaks louder than
spoken to. I'm late, don't care, demand answers to--

slurp cappuccino from white mugs,
ring out the last foam with my left pinkie.
Roll up my jeans, chase little kids across vacant

lots, grab their green and yellow kites. Throw old bread to seagulls,
sprawl my body in the sand at Capitola.
While drinking orange and papaya juice from cartons
I thank myself
for knowing when to leave and when to stay.
I fly on emerald green champagne for breakfast,
gorge oranges at bus stops, kiss my dog on her snout.

You find me in a coral dress--waiting.
Sweep me off, call me yours while I warm your bed,
your coffee, serve it with a smile
or a song if I'm vulnerable and young.

I Don't Understand

how Miles Davis can bring
jazz into my living room,
or how a cat can wind
its tail around itself
then clean with quiet swishing
back and forth.
Sound rises to the ceiling.
I beg it to come down,
its redness and shape
reminds me of silk,
lingerie my husband bought me last week
to celebrate our many years
of being. How wine
the red of pomegranates
can soothe the brain.
I don't understand
a simple sunflower
in a large jar of water,
why the brown velvet center
stalks me, begs me
to pull a seed and let it float
on my hand
before falling.

Font's Point

I told the doctor about Mother's death.
He spoke to my husband:
"Spend time loving her.
Stroke, caress, make love
without penetration."

Flat rock, Font's Point.
We had planned to go there all summer long.

We drive along the sandy road, joy
in the dying day's light, watch
shadows edging dry sagebrush,
uprooted tumbleweeds.

The Desert Badlands
diffuse lingering mauves,
corals and pinks across my body.
A kiss. A sip of Merlot.
Your hand presses my flank against
jagged rocks, the celebrated

first stroke. Rowing the length of me, your fingers
make funnel clouds of breathing skin. You touch belly
button, crotch and inner thigh, use your
hand to circle *what* with
deliberation while my body
bridges these rocks.

I gulp desert wind, then empty my lungs
of the air that dries the yucca's roots.

Intermediate Care

Sugar water,
bag swinging from stand,
his wife in her chair,
he and she on this island

wait for the next blip
to tell them where they are
and where they are going.

No light except
what seeps
across the floor.

Will this long cord
run into the next century?

What will she do
with a rock large enough
to carry to her grave?

The World Over

The children better pray you don't die in the operating room,
because I'll become an embarrassment and succumb
to traveling the world over, sending elephants home

after riding across African savannas wearing plumes
with men twenty years younger, and then some.
The children better pray you don't die in the operating room,

for I'll make love under the banyan trees, consume
the red hibiscus blooms peering through plums,
traveling the world over, sending elephants home

as heirlooms, drink tea with jam, sweep with a banyan broom,
send giraffes to play with their children, and drums.
They better pray you don't die in the operating room.

I'll follow the animal's home to Kate's room, where they'll eat brome
and roam, while I introduce my latest honey with aplomb.
I'll travel the world over, sending elephants home,

then leave for Australia to watch the ink blue bloom,
looking for coral and shells while drinking rum.
The children better pray you don't die in the operating room.
Traveling the world over, sending elephants home.

The Same Color Eyes

"We have the same color eyes, Mom."
Steve stops frying eggplant in the hot oil,
grabs my arm, drags me to our entry mirror.
Pulls my head next to his and points.
"Look, the same color, Mom."
I see what he means. I say hazel.
He says, "Yes, with flecks of amber
and green." He draws me in close
the way I drew him in when he was born.

As a child he traced his fingers,
made lions and giraffes,
squishing clay with his father.

There were times when I didn't know him,
knew only the drugs he used.
I told myself he would get better,
even when I didn't believe
that he would ever want more than
zip-locked bags of marijuana
smoked in hideouts with motorcycle friends.
He drifted. We talked on the phone.
I asked: "Where are you going?"
He hung up.

Years later, we have come to a place
where we sing while eggplants sizzle in olive oil, squirt your arms.
You pull me to our sameness--
eye color and love of eggplant.

Sunday Morning, Port Jefferson, Long Island

I come up behind you,
hold on tight,
wonder if we'll ever hug again--
or if one of us will die
before morning.
Thirty years of marriage,
you age with tenderness,
past forty.

I lean my chin into your shoulder
as I pull you closer to me,
loving the feel of your buns
against my flabby stomach.
You move back and forth
against me.

I rub your shoulder with my chin,
work it back and forth against
your favorite T shirt,
Wyoming blazoned in black and white
across your chest.
My long arms tuck neatly
under yours, their familiar resting place.

Mistress of the Dahlias

"So, I stood in front of the closet door mirrors
naked as I do every morning, combing my hair.
Remember the tree house next door?
How we wondered who went up that rope ladder?"
I nod.
"Well, suddenly I see a flicker,
a slight movement in the mirror,
white, a person's head."
I observe your body, muscular legs
long like the pillars of Shulamite's beloved.
"So I continue combing. But I just had to turn around
and look into the garden. There she was!
with those bent shoulders."
I interrupt--"Our aging Italian mistress
of next door's dahlias? That bent over woman
who plucks and waters daily?"
How many mornings had she climbed
to the top to watch you watch
your nakedness?
You smile.
Your thigh flesh flows toward your scrotum
and upward into the abdomen, your ocean.

Three

Nude Beach

We gain speed, approach the sand where
rosy nipples, dark brown ones, peach-colored,
curvaceous young thighs, larger vein-crossed
older ones, and penises of every length, one lopsided,
whose owners stretch out lazily, seeking grace from above.

He would have persisted all afternoon, if that's
what it took to reach this spot: a place of angular
bodies. Only his does anything for me,
opening to soft breezes.

Later, we pass by a young couple.
"What a beautiful body,
all round, pink and peachy," I exclaim.
Her breasts like soft Elbertas, ripe for the picking,
summers in the San Joaquin. Their color
flows up toward her neck and down her thighs.
He has a proud-peacock thrust to his dark head.
His tail feathers fan out,
each bold eye winking.

More Than Once

Your kiss: a brush on my cheek,
a swallowtail passing. Yellow
and black off my shoulder
as I descend into Squaw Valley.
Or the kind when we've been away for days —
jumping into bed, rolling around in the covers,
finding our lips — quick tongue thrusts
as early morning Anna's hummingbirds
dip into bougainvillea blooms.
Our granddaughter Katie explores
my mouth with her fleshly baby hand, fingers
flat against my gum ridge, feeling every wet
hollow like your tongue's patterns — up and down,
in and around, swishings with their own memory and timing.
I'm staring at the Chagall ceiling in the Paris Opera House
watching red, yellow, and blue figures who defy gravity,
when you plant one on my neck.
The swallowtail's soft brush, a shiver up my thighs
or the long, slow, leisurely, many scattered ones
like dots and dashes in my latest poems
placed so lovingly up and down my body's length
while I'm lying in wait for you. These contain their
own foreknowledge.
And the kitchen kisses, the kind that interrupt bacon
frying and pancake making. I surprise you from
behind, grab you around the waist and tickle your
left ear with one. I give it as a shamrock to insure
this morning's feast will melt on our tongues,
and slip down our throats easily —
like kisses being tasted more than once.

Prostate Surgery

Every three or four days
you would chase me around the bedroom,
playfully tumbling me onto the bed,
grabbing my tits.

I expected this performance,
waited for it, sometimes
acting as if I didn't want it,
but knew I needed it
to make me feel sexy
even if my weight was up,
legs unshaved, hair needed coloring.
You didn't seem to notice.
Primal urges are that way.

Since the surgery,
you do want sex now and then
but not with the same ferocity.
No horniness build up, you say.

I miss being chased.
I always counted on the romp
and the grabbing at…if
everything else went wrong
that week, there would be this
to tell me all was well.

I must remember to tell you
to chase me on schedule,
even if your body fails you.
Check your calendar,
set an alarm clock,
count on your fingers.
When the bell sounds
start the pursuit,
tumble me on the covers,
grab me where I love it.

Our Room Near The Zoo

The lion closes in on the lioness.
I watch the color red
move up your neck to your face.

In our bedroom
you chase me into bed
where we laugh, talk,
and you playfully pin me down.
Let your fingers
slide gently across my breasts.
You listen to my ooo's
and aaah's
while under your body.
Lion pleasure penetrates
the dark.
Our moans travel
out the window, into the garden,
and beyond.
And then it happens outside.
The king of beasts pushes his lioness
to the ground.
Lion growls punctuate
the dark.

Outside Madrid-Mira Flores

"She was an old woman now,
her life had become memories."
  Leslie Marmon Silko

The old man and the old
woman sit in the sun
in front of their stone casita

resting on an oak plank,
balanced on three large
stones, while the sun revels

in play around age lines,
under eyes, over
the bridge of their noses.

The old woman looks down
at her hands whose fingers
nearly touch,

squints
through the intense light
while the old

man gazes at her,
remembering many
such afternoons

when they sat together
this lovingly, their worn
hands resting

in laps, playing with a discarded
pecan shell or leaf. His
cane of sugar cane rests

against stone, propped
there deliberately;
his affection, reserved for

her alone. Cornflower
blue print dress,
blue knit sweater,

felt slippers.
He feels the many stones--
the earths

buff, gray, ochre edges
press into his back; knows
this stone casita grows

out of the land and will
become the land again.

The gaps between planks
on the oak door suggest
a young woman's willowy

dance: her shadow etched
fine as pencil lines moves
across these boards.

He gazes at her cheek, watches
the sun curve round her
hands like a welcome cat

come to play. He and she
a corner for light
to cup and gather.

Hailing A Cab

we head for M and Wisconsin.
My friend scoots across the vinyl seat, smiles
at the driver and asks: "How has your day been?"
"Beautiful," he intones, "lots of business,
lots of tips to take home to the wife."
"Do you ever take a day off ? " she asks him.
"No, I love to work. When I'm home, she nags."
"Why are you sitting in that chair?
Mow the lawn, clean the garage etc., etc."

He pulls up a canvas bag. "I bring food
with me: fruit, a sandwich, park the cab,
sit by the water, eat my orange, watch the ducks,
enjoy the sun."

"Do you like poetry?" she asks. "My friend here
is a poet." "I don't like them," he says. "They make
something into what it's not. They lie and tell me
the sun's rays turn into gold in my pocket."

"You should hear my friend's poems," she persists.
"You'd like them."
Her smile tells me where she's headed.
I've never given a reading in a cab before.
I pull "Outside Madrid…" from my purse.
He'll understand this old woman who has only her memories.
"If it's bad, I double your fare; if it's good, it stays the same."

As sound circles the cab's interior,
his right ear cocks toward me, eyes straight ahead
on the light about to change. The old woman's blue stockings,
cornflower dress, casita that will be there after they are gone.
By the time the light turns red, I have his full attention.
"He and she/make a corner for light/to cup and gather."
His face changes, muscles soften, sadness
lines the ridges like the age lines of the couple in the poem.

The last syllable flows off my tongue.
He speeds ahead of an adjacent truck.
"I owe you something," he says. His cheek contorts.
I lean back against the warm seat,
let the old couple breathe through me.

Focused Light

Remember the narrow strip, Grandpa,
two feet between your white garage wall
and the neighbor's fence?
Just enough distance for tomato seedlings
to expand in the heat.

You scatter cosmos seeds near where Grandma
hangs laundry, damp clothes fly out all summer
over hundreds of pink and lilac blooms.
You pinch cuttings in Berkeley's rose garden,
sometimes a single leaf, to grow
Tropicana roses near your pear tree.
Later fuchsias, carnations and stock
bloom up the steep driveway,
spill over the porch, extend every corner.
After our walks, flower dreams recur for days.
Dinner plate dahlias whirl in space,
petunias call me to press the earth
down firm around their roots.

We eat these tomatoes whole.
Juice drips down our chins, our fingers,
after each bite.
Tell my children, your grandchildren,
how you grew these tomatoes in that narrow space,
between the white wall and the neighbor's fence.
Teach me what to plant, and how to plant it.

We Have To Walk A Long Way
in the world to know the truth of certain things--Pablo Neruda

to know why rain purples
the iris stem
and not the poppy's;
to know my lover's kiss
on my forehead:
something I can count on;
to know the leather strap
clasped between
forefinger and thumb
feels smooth like the skin of a lime;
to know that snow
in a village in Vermont
glistens while my eyes are closed;
to know how the smiles of children
equal half moons placed
on my lips
by the moon giver;
to know that red nail polish
gives off light on a winter
afternoon, enough to fill
the clear pitcher by my bed;
to know pigeons,
and seagulls walking on the sand,
parading themselves
so I can watch and imitate;
to know why my grandson
stands so tall on the wooden stairs,
his red winter hat on
inside out, his upward strength
the shape of his manhood to come;
to know that listening

catches a duck's glide
lightly in the ear
as purple syllables
correspond to sibilant
and licorice;
to know how to walk a long way in the snow,
ask directions from skaters
on a neighboring pond
who glide into twilight
and beyond;
to know
ice crunching underfoot
and air breathed in
where it catches
and almost chokes me
into wondering
if truth is a long way
into the world: a path
that glistens up ahead
but never lets me
slow down
and catch my breath
near the iris
in the rain.

Indian Head
for Lois

"I've died but you are still living!"
This marble face is still living, if rock lives.
Today October sun heats his Indian profile,
white light burns forehead, eye socket, upper lip.

Metamorphic face scans the desert.
Climbing up, we can see rock bands, schist,
marble, layers under pressure,
like husbands and sons who change us into who we are.

This light reveals gray brown Bighorn sheep.
Back on the desert floor, ocotillo blooms cover
the ground like tiny hummingbirds who whirred their last--
a wreckage that burns into Fall.

A desert stream flows near us.
On parched grass, enclosed by mountains,
we sit next to each other telling our stories--
Watch! Nothing can stop this light's revelation.

after Jane Cooper

Lackawanna

Your sleep canoe glides silently
past an old Indian village--
your wooden dream paddle pulls
water back, reveals shadows
of tangled sea greens crisscrossing.
Each pull back on the oars plows
the canoe's point toward the sun's slow
rising above your native place.
A lean too far to right or left can tip
this bark and lose the early dream.
No chance to gather up those shadows.

House of the Treetops

Hana, Maui, Hawaii

We're sleeping in a jungle
where leafy Mostare trees sway
to ancient Hawaiian songs:

rain splatters
on fiberglass roof,
runs down corrugated folds,

drips off edges. A bird whirs
its wings in the tree behind us.
We can't see it. The sun tries

to peek through clouds to our right.
A piece of blue comes
through an opening formed

by towering cumulus
which separate at one point.
The shape of Maui:

two islands linked by a land bridge.
Mosquito netting draped over our bed
filters all we see. A grass mat

hangs on a narrow wall:
cone shapes replicate volcanoes.
A zinging, buzzing sound

mingles a parrot's and a horny cat's.
Some birds I can't name.
Then the usual chirping of house finches,

cardinals, and the constant screeching
of mynahs everywhere
on this island: here to mark a stone

wall, there a path to something,
or the way up
to the next waterfall. Now a louder song

in answer to the Eastern cardinal's "twilight, twilight."
Branches sway, we play in our bed,
pillows propped, watching the weather change.

Early sun isolates the Mostare green.
A tree I've barely seen
these past seven nights
grows through our bedroom.

On the Vine

They lie alongside each other…
Two string beans
immobile
before the farmer's wife picks them,
while early morning
still glazes
their skin.
He shifts on the vine,
edges closer
to the curved line
of her.

In The Desert

The evening of the time change,
we made love under an October sky,
set our clocks to shorter days from longer,
longer nights from shorter.
During sweet release
we watched
something shoot across the sky
leaving "not stars" you said,
"only dust."
We fell asleep,
woke just before the sun
turned the smoke tree
into an object of burning.
"Look, the dipper is standing on end,"
you said.   "Yes." I whispered.
Water pours upward
to meet the sky.
We snuggle back down,
pull our bodies into each other,
alongside each one's knowing.

The Owl

His white heart-shaped face.
His eyelid open.
This owl stare finds both of you unafraid.
Hushed by his gaze.
You keep looking
for something which will not speak
from a place two have known.

Two crawl
Up piled leaves--
Lean into
these owl silences.

And they are free
in those dark eyes.
They are a tree cavity
holding owlishness.

They remember to cherish,
to confide some lack
between themselves.
Something light-colored
and nocturnal
keeps them at a safe distance.

Four

Fiesta

religious celebration featuring pagan dances
addressed to Christian saints a deep pink
bluer lighter stronger than average coral

six foot redhead a poet fiesta
when asked to describe my friend

happiness or poetry

waiting to
love gratitude and mardi gras
she answers when asked what she wants

she writes on gourmet pizza menu
basil and meathead to order

when reading her poem *my naked husband*
color rises up her cheeks   a fiesta
of deep pink to stronger than average coral

she dances in processions
on the streets of Barcelona and Seville
knows she moves like the Christian saints
head high feet firmly planted
the mountain pose they taught her in yoga
bluer than blue--pink robe
rope belt
swings her red hair *auburn with hints of copper*
she calls it
she marches all six feet of herself through Barcelona
a poet fiesta   love gratitude
this woman who kisses goldfish
how her granddaughter taught
this pleasure
mardi gras
heyday or jubilee

Flamenco Dancer

She wakes her two children
who sleep with her in the family caverna.
Their father joined a gypsy caravan
bound for Morocco.
Isabella and Angelina eat warm bread,
drink hot chocolate, dress for school.

She inspects their nails before
the nuns do. Abuela
cares for the girls after school.
Cave dances, eager tourists,
she sees them in her mind's eye
clapping and staring,

her hands raised in the Flamenco pose,
clicking her fingers
in time to her long, loosely draped body,
her electric response to the guitarra.
She hates their stares, feels like a parrot
on show behind bars.

At the corner café she eats tapas,
    drinks wine after work.
Her voice rattles like parched gravel
    in the corner courtyards
where the wind blows fiercely,
    from the Sierra Nevada's.

After a bottle, she hears her own
contralto voice, a resonant sound,
remembers resting her head
    on her mother's warm stomach.
Most evenings, she smells alcohol,
    cigarettes, and sweat.

Her clothes reek of her,
   not washed for a week.
During her showers, local boys gawk
 over corrugated steel.
I am old wax, she remembers,
 melted down, nothing left to burn.

She imagines her parents strewing
   roses on her grave, lighting
candles to honor the dead. The girls
wear necklaces with tiny gold
crosses. I am a turnip she broods, anchored to the earth,
   an enormous bat suspended.

She meets him at the market,
   buys pan, chorizo,
bolts of flannel smelling of the sun.
   He drinks espresso at a round table.
Older, grizzled, he catches her
off guard with a word.

She carries her black coffee
to his table.
I often come here for Mother's flannel.

The fabric of the old, he says,
     hard to keep warm
during the nights.

Are you a dancer?

Yes. We dance for the tourists in Grenada.
He notes the swing to her long hair,
her toe tapping on the floor's sunny tile.

She later remembers his remark:
   "…hard to keep warm,"
feels the girls' arms heavy with sleep
reach around her in the dark.

What Is Lost
(a conversation between sister-in-laws)

I haven't told anyone yet
except for Pete. Ache everywhere,
fear it's in my bones, can't stand.

You stretch out on the sun porch couch,
wiggle your toes, extend, rest,
extend, rest.

"We'll get through this together,"
Pete said to me the other day.
It's not "we," I told him.
It's my disease, you can't help me.

I admit no words, move towards you
on the couch, give a hug, feel your body,
thin as a sail propelling you towards death.
I almost believe I can reach through scant bones,
wasted away muscle tissue, to touch what's lost:
two perfect breasts.

I'm just a kid again,
a flat-chested three year old,
everything gone, even my nipples.

You raise your blouse,
underneath a T shirt
with two pockets,
cotton falsies stuck in,
a suggestion of fullness,
something almost round.

Studying The Hair On His Arms
While Driving To Home Depot

"Hair," you awaken her to curlicues,
those half circles of light she dreams about.
Some red, the Norwegian in him,
some white, marking his years after 60.
A curl reminds her of how they sleep curled
into each other. You "hair" are lover driving
her sex towards his. You are the "curly bear"
she strokes at night for comfort. At twelve,
she painted curlicues on her closet wall in pink and purple,
cut her nails for the first time. Old nails fell in half circles of 3,
made her yearn for the completed ones of 8.

Light illuminates each curlicue while his arm rests
on the steering wheel. These arm hairs ignite, stroke her,
arc into playful curls of the mind. Hers wants to curl back
on itself, hook some tendril of thought, bring it to the surface,
into the Jeep Wrangler, to ride with them for almost forty years.
She likes summer best. He wears tank tops, exposes places
for the sun to rest, to light up. In winter, she reaches under his sleeve,
lets her fingers play a game with curls and warmth like watching sunlight
pool under pine trees. She caresses his arm, a gesture toward lovemaking.

Some nights they give into fatigue, prefer to make their own curlicues,
stroke each other like cats, postpone until tomorrow A.M.
when bodies will rise "fresh" like loaves from the oven.

Some days lightening flashes!
Other days, energy must be counted out like buttons from mother's button box.

Hay waits to be harvested while mice with tiny feet pile up for a nap together.

Direct oblong glances, red hair in full sunlight,
the shape and twist of "Yes."

"Waiter There's A Hair In My Margarita"

something I pull from crushed ice
and tequila, hold up to
strong afternoon sun.

Waiter, did you lose something
from your upper lip?" What did I do
to deserve this small gift of Mexican hospitality
presented with such foam and circumstance...

"Waiter there's a hair in my margarita,
your lost symbol of male virility,
giving something over to a feminine domain.

Is this yours.?
A device to measure how much tequila I can drink."
When I reach it where it almost drags the bottom
surely I'll know enough to climb stone steps
and stagger home from beach and lunch.

What might I lose that someone else might find:
my red wig, rose-colored glasses or the afternoon sun?

I Lose My Breath Climbing the Hills

of San Miguel de Allende, carry
clementines, a satchel, three books
and a picture of you.

I
I lose my penultimate line, the one
that spells "shadow," your
body beside the bougainvillea,
San Miguel's uneven skyline,
curves which round into the ground.

Then there's the final word, the one
caught at the back of my throat.
Disregard, acknowledge,
settle the loss I feel,
a glance at your aging body,
our time together,
three quarters gone and passing.

II
I search for words
three quarters gone and passing,
our time together,
aging bodies I know,
sideways glance at yours
to settle this loss
caught at the back of my throat,
the final word,
"the ground," the line along,

it's rounding down from your curves
above San Miguel's uneven skyline,
bougainvillea on the rooftop,
the shade your body casts as you lean against.
I lose my penultimate shadow,
your picture and three books,
clementines, a satchel.
San Miguel de Allende,
climbing its hills
I lose my breath.

All Of The Mothers Are Dying

My friend's in early July,
his last Christmas.
Some too young,
others too old to know better.
All of the mothers are dying.
Some from Alzheimer's,
others from brain tumors.
His father calls to say "Come quickly."
Hers says "Take your time, she'll
linger for awhile, but plan the funeral."
Some stay alive for birthdays, and weddings,
keep silent about when they plan to go.

Walking The Dog And The Goldfish
As observed from the backseat of a Subaru

"You walk the dog."
"No, I'll put the kids to bed."
"No, I'll do that while you walk the damn dog.
You wanted it, I didn't."
She hears her parents' arguing.
Eight-and-three-quarters girl:
"Married people sleep in the same bed,
eat the same food, dress together,
can't they agree on something?"

You want to find out what happened
in that home ask the youngest child.
Five-and-three-quarters boy:
"idiots."
Webster's: fails to exhibit normal or usual
sense, mental age not exceeding three years,
a clown, unlearned.

Practice making decisions: Go to the store,
buy a dog or two goldfish. Fish for something
in each other's eyes.
"There's that damn dog barking again."
"Stop him."
"He's not my dog."

Sleep, eat, dress together.
Agree on something.
Take a walk in the rain,
forget your burdens and your games.
Step out together into puddles, hop like
children, first one foot, then the other.
How to learn the word "another."
Keep moving, step into ponds
reflecting rain boots,
kids in yellow slickers.
Swing your arms like idiots who walk a dog.

Glide

To move in an effortless manner without apologizing
to your children for anything
to slide your body to the side, an overarching
alive, to occur, pass imperceptibly
this light almost Spring snowfall
still *gliding* across my vision line after all these hours
the way I can leave a room without you noticing
your head might lift imperceptibly
a nod to my *glide* away from
the newspaper guarding your face
we learn the foxtrot--hold
our frame of arms tight--
my back a lean into your palm
expect to *glide* soon "keep the frame tight"
the instructor cautions "or she will go off,
create her own steps" your speech
glides consonants or vowels together
makes something I can barely understand
syllables I meant to listen to
for a smooth effortless move I might
undertake soon
my own vocabulary for *"glide"*

Anza Borrego Desert Afternoon
For Dixie

Red-shouldered hawk on a wire,
another on the ground.
Two phainopepla, glossy
black, fly from a creosote
bush, roadrunner clack
clacks, I doze poolside.
Coyotes squeal, bark,
howl over their meaty repast.
Ocotillo drips red flames
down, something to paint
tomorrow. Crickets click
in the heat--"a bad omen
to kill one"--say the Chinese.
I dream three palms, then paint
them fluorescent orange, lime
green and fuchsia. Roots spring
up in mountain cracks.
Anza Borrego Desert Afternoon
rests on the table beside me.

Woman Looks At Trevi Fountain

sees her reflection, faces him, throws coins,
arm up when he takes the picture.
Only the fish knows how many coins she throws.
This woman looks at columns in the forum, remembers
when she walked among them twenty-five years ago
with husband, two sons, and a stray calico cat.
Now, she looks at same columns behind steel fences;
they bar her from touching and leaning.
Her smile a coliseum curve, her eyes: square holes for windows.
A woman eats banana and orange from a street vendor.

Later she waits behind many women in the toilette, squats over a hole.
She can't remember why she ordered spaghetti and clams,
fettuccini vongole. She knows it won't taste like her father's.
"Fantastico," she later tells the waiter who says "No,"
to the parmesan, "covers up the fish flavor." Tiny clams,
their swirled green shells float in wine, garlic, olive oil.
This woman pulls out bits with her finger tips, later waits
in an empty train for two hours, stares at red poppies
which grow tall between train tracks.

At the villa, she asks for a "room with a view."
"Sorry Madam, they're all booked." She didn't arrive sooner,
even the partial views are none, moves into the room
with sparrow-covered trees outside. No view, constant bird chirping.
She loves their Oh-dear-me, oh-dear-me's, descending whistle notes.
feeds birds raw oats from her breakfast table.
he came to write poetry late,
didn't finish the letter to the man on death row, palm trees
on the villa grounds sway, clouds keep blocking out the sun,
fronds keep clicking like mother's fingers snapped
to make children obey. This woman listens to palm blades
crisscross, fan out the breeze above her head.

What will they do for money when her husband quits work?
Maybe she'll have to waitress, or sell their home to their son.
Their son-in-law wants to divorce their lovely daughter.
This woman smiles at a small boy who waves back, blows her a kiss.

Can't let her disappointments go, continues to stare
at the clicking, clacking palm fronds, swaying and sawing
the wind, hears bells from the villa's terrace ring for lunch,
she'll eat indoors or out if the sun on her back can sink
into muscle tissue through jacket and blouse, if the laundry
hanging from the nearby apartments swings and sways all afternoon.
How she came to be so young at sixty one.

She crosses her fingers in prayer.
The sun keeps going behind a cloud.

Venezia

The woman came out to water her geraniums
after I reached my sexual peak, rolled over,
sighed. She continued to water both boxes.

We had flung the louvered windows open wide
to late afternoon sun on clay tiled roofs,
three floors above the street at the Hotel Capri.
"Look at the view," I exclaimed while he watched
the naked me watch Venezia's early Spring sky.
A sparrow landed on the chimney,
tiles baked in late afternoon.

Fahrenheit Fifty-One
Gale Meadow Lake, Vermont

Legs, inner thighs, and clitoris
begin to numb; I ponder the difference

between an orgasm and a mid-October swim,
immerse myself into the water fearlessly,

the way I let my body slide
toward my husband's fingers,

wait for him to awaken me.
He mats down grass beside

this lake, leans back, surveys the water's
deep blue-green, his Seattle baseball cap askew.

Cold freezes bones, soaks into skin,
numbs the mind. Sex awakens it

to roam primeval forests chased
by fisher cats and wolves.

Five

Dutiful Husband

He kisses my nipples every morning,
sings them awake, ignites them
with his wet, cool tongue until
pinkish-brown flames heat up,
stand on end in obeisance.

Moist, his tongue's tip blesses,
pays tribute to,
acclaims, compliments,
gives a bouquet, glorifies,
celebrates, sings praises
to, flatters.

His words in the early dawn:
"…beautiful, such a delicate flavor,
so like strawberries and cantaloupe."
Playful morsels for my mind
to suck on all day.
He returns at 6 p.m.
to lullaby them to sleep.

Lunch With My Therapist
(Six Years Later)

I meet you running
across the bank parking lot
in a tuxedo suit trimmed in red,
longer blond hair than I remember,
waving like the flag
of some forgotten country.
We have returned from a journey
behind a closed door. You helped me
wipe away grit from sandstorms,
chopped away the underbrush with your machete.

Here we are again sitting face-to-face.
I'd forgotten how funny we'd been together.
We eat outdoors at the Breeze Café,
order low fat capps, shrimp and bean wraps,
ask and answer questions for an hour.

 "You're still crazy," you intone
later in the parking garage.
"Still on the raw side of wacky,"
I say, "I paid you to change me."
"I want a refund."
"I can't, I spent it all living in Ireland."
"At least you could take me next time you go," I beg.
You wave, cruise away in your butterscotch Datsun.

Hotel Posada de Las Monjas

Last night I heard crying on the deck
above me, uncontrollable weeping
alternating with loud disco music
from the bar where a mounted and stuffed
toro head hangs. This anguish continued
while someone scraped chairs
across gravel, then more weeping.

I wondered if it was Sarah. Her son,
a famous sculptor from Italy,
fell off his roof before Christmas.
Died. She's found some women
who will comfort her,
huddle around while she pours
out her misery to the stars--tears
fell, seeped, plopped between her fingers
onto the patio roof where they lay underneath
the sky, evaporated slowly--while the moon's sickle
encircled as much darkness as its finite curve
could hold.

I Do Not Travel Lightly

instead I pack all of my possessions,
hanging like my grandmother's pendulum
breasts from my chest, shimmering icons I can't
leave to chance or mountain tops, a library
including Neruda to Rilke, W.D. and E.D.
The dromedary balances a large basket
on his hump: stone necklaces, dangle earrings,
a bracelet loaded with yesterday's charms.

I carry my griefs and regrets in leather satchels
stitched to my body. The forgotten years:
silk turbans, black, sea green, wrap around my head.

I coil my longings about my waist like snakes,
carry my dreams in wooden hampers: a book
of poems still to be published, a wife for my youngest son.
Around my ankles in coiled leather:
the days that march by when we have nothing to say
to each other.

Small Ecstasies

Mr. and Mrs. Cardinal feed
outside my kitchen window.
She eats from the ground
while he balances his regal red
on the feeder's edge, cocks his head,
watches for what moves while singing.

Bringing coffee to my love, I whisper in his ear:
"It is here," while he keeps sleeping.
Know he will rise soon, watch the cardinals
with me: my second ecstasy

Late afternoon, the sun drops low
behind the trees' half-circle, winter gold trunks
near last season's pumpkins.
Before sleep, your silky arm
encircles my waist, enfolds me.

A Birthday for Amy

He made a restaurant for her in his garden,
draped off any view of the street,
devised a canopy with sheets,
placed thirty-two candles in a circle for this occasion.
For love and friendship he often
brought twelve red roses, meadow-sweet,
to highlight almost any event.
First he pointed out the moon,

a loaf of sourdough bread on a black plate.
Artichokes and lasagna were followed
by a question: He asked if she was ready for her gift. She replied,
later. I can't wait (he meant to delineate.)
Will you marry me? he asked, placing a ring on her finger.
She whispered, are you sure?

He Married Her For The Second Time

Under an arbor
among peonies and irises
before he remembered to rescue himself

The charcoal moon settled above the lower mountains,
curve of lettuce leaves in a wooden bowl.
They wrote their love letters in twilight,
dipped into love's ink,
red for burning,
hot□what they wrote:
Spanish words for pain,
breath coming hard and fast,
her leg,
his hand,
Mexico's love story,
his arms around her hips,
embraces in the Jardine,
twilight's dusky tomate.
Bird choruses ceased, sound lingered in the jacarandas
mixed with cebolla, and lechuga.

He wrote his devotion in charcoal
on her palm,
threw stones,
forgave her
for this burning,
leaping into fire,
singing,
arms and hands,
soft Spanish contours,
shapes of the moon
reflected in the Guadalquiver,
Mexico's river,
where stones marked space,
how long it took to jump from one to the other.

A Rooster in the Rain

persistent as the hours, the urge to
signal each one so often: 12,
2, 4, 5 a.m., myself trying to sleep
a decent sleep while rain
pelts our roof, the wet a reminder of you, next to me, but not
today, we're on separate vacations,
but I remember my semi-lust
in former, cooler, less-light days
when the only decent sound
locked itself and love inside
our son's peony strewn garden where
young girls played flute duets our 40th anniversary.

I Locked My Elbow

showed the old Mexican fisherman
my persistent muscles, how
I reeled in that huge Sierra fish,
the one they cooked from hardness
to decent flakiness so often at Suzy's,
grilled with garlic, ajo—according to our
specifications. Eating it a reminder
of the wet, you next to me in Suzy II,
the restaurant's boat for fishing trips.
We sat side by side; I leaned into the day.
The slap, slap sound of waves
against the boat's side. You with
ease crowed like the rooster in his
semi-lust, cockadoodledoing before one a.m.

Something Rounder

for Steve and Janet

Red and yellow peaches,
"mellow fruitfulness,"
overflows the glass heirloom
fruit bowl. Janet said,
"I want a yellow kitchen
in our new home."
Lemons grace the bowl's edge,
rest against blue watercolor.
Fruit nestles deep inside
the glass concavity,
waits for the ripening.
Marriage--a union--
peaches and lemon
sweet and tart
   make a peach pie
add cinnamon for spice
You two embrace, cling to keep steady,
hold onto something rounder,
what you will make together,
layering slices, each one curving
into the next.

Departure Of The Blue Heron

We took our usual walk
my friend and I.
Saw the neighbor on his hands and knees
push down one brick after another.
Rounding the corner, she gasped,
pulled my shoulder into her line of vision.
We saw him rise abruptly
from his watery place.
You couldn't call it a pond,
just a spot where water collects.
He took off…dark blue up!
Left us so fast we weren't sure
he had been there at all.

Baby, we've been waiting for you.
Mama patting her stomach,
Daddy listening to your moves
with ear pressed flat,
now suits up in white with blue cap
to watch you come caked in the vestiges
of your former life,
chalky overcoat spattered with blood.
Later behind glass, you stretch your limbs,
a victory salute, the inverted spread
of the heron's legs
as he rises up
into an August evening.

A Shrine To Summer

See the big rock over there on our deck,
the one you dug from the "lake,"
or Newton Pond as the locals call it.

This rock stays put these days,
clean beside two straws,
an empty plastic coke bottle,
three smaller rocks,
several leaves that drifted in
since you left us to go home to Mom and Dad.

You insisted on lugging the largest rock
you could find home from the beach,
carefully cradling it in your arms
like a baby, adding weight to memory,
our long canoe ride to the island.
"I'm taking this to your house, Grammy;
you take the smaller ones, and the water bottle."

You arranged them carefully on the floor boards,
laughingly told your fish story to our friend who came for lunch.
"I caught an eighteen incher. It almost pulled me out of the boat."

Three days later, I drink coffee here beside your shrine
to summer, love's positioning of the season. Early rays
glance off the biggest rock.
Two sticks/plastic bottle rest exactly as you left them.

They enshrine a memory in our minds,
bless the days before you return to us.

Six

Southern California Women

Scene I:
*Camera focuses on an orange/red sun rising behind
the freeway overpass near the LA airport. Alberta
checks in her luggage curbside.*

Alberta: Damn, I forgot to have my ears pierced!

Scene II:
*Flashback to the patio outside Café Pinguini,
Gwenn's tenth anniversary. She enters,
laughs a loud, neighing horse laugh.*

Gwenn: (to guests including Alberta)
Inscribe your name on my picture
with Andrew. I love Roman columns,
white space, gifts in the corner: blown glass
coral roosters, yellow and purple lizard
from Oaxaca. I chose mini pizzas for appetizers,
fresh tomatoes, basil, mushrooms and cheese.
(Gwenn commands.) Find the table with your picture!

Waiter holds out a plate to Gwenn and Alberta.

Alberta: Look, there's Bob and I staring at a mountain of ceviche in Ensenada!

Gwenn: This party, what a trip! I love people with names I don't remember
like Katrina, and Natalia, my Russian girlfriend with navel and tongue piercing.
Husband works for the Secret Service; she has a life of her own. She met him when
she
worked as a call girl, wore red mini-skirts, blew half a million dollars living large.

Alberta: Gwenn, remember the Christmas party in Borrego, you told us to howl
at the moon? Give us a moon howl now!

Gwenn: whoooooooo, whooooOOOO, WHOOOOOOOO (in a crescendo)
Did you see the fairies with breasts howling at the moon over Manhattan Beach?
My Russian girl friend howls at the Crimean moon, drinks her history with vodka,

eats sturgeon eggs destined for extinction. Dreams about millions of Russians with no names, dead.

Scene III:
After the party, Alberta and Gwenn relax in Gwenn's hot tub.

Gwenn: I need someone to hand me grapes and peel them.
Your voice lulls me when you read "Ode To My Breasts."

Alberta reads from her poem:

> Hips may be wacky,
> Too pear shaped, but you
> two stay taut, pointing me
> in the right direction,
> so I know my body
> still yearns and churns.

Gwenn: And the one about the fairies who painted themselves in fuchsias and greens.
I took a Demerol, and then your voice did it all. Words dropped, pebbles splashed, pulled me down like gravity.

Scene IV
At the Los Angeles Airport where Alberta prepares to board.

Alberta: It takes five holes to "live large."
Damn, I forgot to have my ears pierced.

Ode To My Breasts

I saw you on my x-rays today,
last year's mammograms.
You dog-faced boobs
with capillaries exposed,
swirling, interrelated lines
on a charcoal sketch.

You, who nourished two babies,
boys who couldn't get enough,
smiled and looked up
from their gorging,
drank again, then slept.

Your dog-faces worshipped
by my husband for thirty-seven years.
I call him "the breast man,"
insatiable like his two boys.

Your profiles:
firm, uplifted, still pointing
straight ahead with candor
after all these years.

I can count on you.
Hips may be wacky,
too pear shaped, but you
two stay taut, pointing me
in the right direction,
so I know my body
still yearns and churns.

Your dog faces smiling
as only dogs can.

Early Morning Flight

I'm 14C, you're 14B.
The plane is taxiing
and all I can think about
is the hair on your arm
rubbing my forearm.
It tickles.
I move my left elbow.
Where can I place it?
I want to escape
this gentle brush of hair,
but back my arm goes.
Our hairs create
their own magnetic dance.
Up your arm goes
to hold your paper,
rubbing hairs again.
We take off and climb,
connect through follicles.
I sense your musing
behind black and white,
content to be left alone
during flight time.
My arm is a cat
arching its back
on fences and tree trunks.
My cat-back-arm
doesn't have to look
for places to rub.
You move your hairs
up and down,
down and up.
You look satisfied
rubbing hairs with me;
and why shouldn't you?

We Hold The Mountain Pose

While Our Yoga Teacher Tells Her Story:

.   *I painted this bougainvillea*
my first afternoon in San Miguel,

chose a tube of paint labeled
"Opera," a shade of hot pink,

a flush to complement old ceramic tiles,
and sky, azure or ultramarine.

The next afternoon, two men came, carried sharp machetes.
After four hours, they left my patio covered

in dark green leaves, petals that filled in the blanks
between the uneven bricks,

pink curving upwards towards the sun.
Bougainvillea branches that covered

the roof and back wall were gone, cut down
before we left for Queretaro.

"Thank you ladies for listening, now complete
your meditation, rise, deep breathe, 'namaste'."

I will see the teacher this afternoon across from my patio,
picking up deep pink petals with her fingers,
sweeping the ancient bricks clean
while I sip café Americano.

My Finger Lies Quiet Along Your Stem

I picked you, Spanish iris.
Your color reminds me of yesterday.
I failed to notice you on my afternoon walk--
your deep violet falls and honey-scented breath.
Your narrow, green leaves,
where you stand among lilies in wild gardens.
I trace the velvet softness of your petals,
veined lines, fluted edges of my wanderings.

Resting On The Academy Library Lawn

A place to be, to hear,
to weave the mind's reed baskets,
fill them with Bach's flute sonatas
wafting from the library windows.

Yeats heard these sounds
"in the deep heart's core." How deep,
how far in to find the loss, which one,
which glass bowl does rainwater fill
to the brim? We dance to escape from,
to loosen our heart strings,
or apron strings.

Rest now, lie down, look up,
see sky filter something you can't
calculate. How many leaves make
an umbrella to shelter you and him?

Adolescents perfume their mating dance,
butterflies do it in mid-air,
we dance the mating dance of the eyes,
a finely tuned balance.
Tree limbs sway above our heads
where we walk soundless,
feeling arced wood beneath
our bare feet as we spin out
into color the shape of canopy,
green, linden blue, yellow, trees.

Green light spills over
into summer's shadow.
How many linden trees will it take
to fill your life's container
to the lip with leaves?

My Belly Speaks

What did you eat to paunch me out, make
a gathered bag out of me? I hum music
lovelier than frogs croaking, my longings
rise up to the keeper of the stars.
You touch me, call me, Belly, ask me why I am rounder
or more slack. I am soft and warm. Your hubby
loves to rest his head on me while watching
T.V., then ignores me to fondle breasts and thighs.
I carried two babies for you, rocked them equidistant
between your pelvic bones, a natural hammock.
During labor, the nurses couldn't find my contractions.
They said: "Belly too flat and hard."
I heard your babies cry as they escaped in a watery swoosh,
later fattened up to make pillows for grandkids
who called me "Grammy's Flabby Stomach."

You examine me in the antique mirror every
evening. After listening to Oprah, I tell you,
"You Go Girl." Some clothes you try on don't flatter
my rising mound. I counsel: "Choose things that fall
over edges with grace. I long for my youthful, flat
board-like shape. Your husband kisses my soft,
belly flesh. Each kiss becomes a star.

Philosophers say I am the seat of all emotion,
a twinge, a gut reaction to his nasty words
last night, or baby's first lunge in my amniotic fluid.
I am, Belly, keeper of life blossoms, belly, as balloon
holding air, spirits rising from my heat, strength, sex.

Forty Dollars a Bun

I see the price tag hanging
from your Banana Republic slacks,
the black silk ones
you think you look so good in
except for a small sag
where, as you say,
your thighs are *so thin,*
or should I say *muscular.*
I'll have my tailor
alter these slacks next week.
I can't believe my eyes!
You of the minute by minute
perfection. Never a crumb,
wisp of lint, or drop of anything
to break this altogether, overall
total look. I see it and know
I have something on you!
This tag hangs down between
your bun cleavage.
There it is: "Banana Republic
$80.00."
You are a $40.00 a bun woman.
A total one--
whole grained, full brained,
neither looking to the right or left.
Whole grained bread
all your life must have done it.
The right brain
must have let the left one
slip up. Not enough attention
to details to destroy this evidence
of bun priciness.
They're awfully small and compact
for this hefty tag. Barely enough
in two to squeeze with one large hand.

They do have a nice curve,
flowing out slightly
from your lower back,
and rounding into your thighs.
I'm not complaining,
you say. *Heavens, I've run*
my buns off for these.

No More Mine

I realized as I sat among the reeds
waiting for the one I loved
that she was both body and soul to me, but no more mine for that.
                    Old Norse Legend

She curled her back
to my stomach
her breath to my breath
eased her sleep canoe
away from day's edge

If we could be
Two ripe persimmons
A juicy sweetness commingling

No more mine than
koi breaking water
or steam from a meadow
with stars at our feet

Underwater Grace

I float above the coral reefs
in the waters off Kauai,
glide toward bloater fish, sea bass,
white against ocean's blue.
These silent bodies move
with dolphin grace in channels
known only to themselves.
Watching bodies feed makes me ask
if I can dignify my life with smooth,
curved lines, momentary stops,
side glances at obstacles.

Printed in the United States
37276LVS00006B/343-498

9 780890 023815